GOOD GRIEF! CHARLIE BROWN DOODLES

Create and Complete Pictures with the Peanuts Gang
BY CHARLES M. SCHULZ

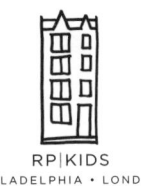

RP|KIDS
PHILADELPHIA · LONDON

Copyright © 2012 by Peanuts Worldwide, L.L.C.

All rights reserved under the Pan-American and International Copyright Conventions

Printed in China

This book may not be reproduced in whole or in part, in any form or by any means, electronic or mechanical, including photocopying, recording, or by any information storage and retrieval system now known or hereafter invented, without written permission from the publisher.

Books published by Running Press are available at special discounts for bulk purchases in the United States by corporations, institutions, and other organizations. For more information, please contact the Special Markets Department at the Perseus Books Group, 2300 Chestnut Street, Suite 200, Philadelphia, PA 19103, or call (800) 810-4145, ext. 5000, or e-mail special.markets@perseusbooks.com.

ISBN 978-0-7624-4448-9
Library of Congress Control Number: 2011937852

9   8   7   6   5   4   3   2
Digit on the right indicates the number of this printing

Art adapted by Ryan Hayes
Cover and interior design by Ryan Hayes
Edited by Lisa Cheng
Typography: Typography of Coop

Running Press Kids
An Imprint of Running Press Book Publishers
A Member of the Perseus Books Group
2300 Chestnut Street
Philadelphia, PA 19103–4371

Visit us on the web!
www.runningpress.com
www.snoopy.com

Watch out, Charlie Brown!
What is Lucy holding this time?

What did Sally receive in the mail?

Linus and Marcie found treasure on the way to school! What does it look like?

Lucy can't catch the baseball!
Draw her a trusty glove.

What is Charlie Brown looking for in the cookie jar?

It's Snoopy's dinnertime! Fill his bowl.

Breakfast looks yummy!
What are Linus and Lucy having?

Linus and Snoopy built a tower out of blocks!
How high does it go?

Rerun is blowing lots of bubbles!
Doodle some big ones.

Linus and Sally have built an army of snowmen! Finish drawing them.

Pig-Pen looks a little too clean.
Give him some dust and grime.

Snoopy and Charlie Brown noticed something on the golf course! What is it?

Rain, rain, go away! Draw umbrellas for Marcie and Peppermint Patty so they don't get wet!

What is Rerun drawing?

Eek! What is scaring Charlie Brown?

What is Sally carrying?

Nice toss, Charlie Brown! Where is his Frisbee?

What new land does the Flying Ace see?

Lucy is playing doctor today! Who is coming to see her? How much does she charge?

Schroeder is playing the piano,
but he needs some musical notes!

Caution! What kind of roadwork is being done?

Charlie Brown and Snoopy are daydreaming.
What kind of tree are they leaning against?

What is chasing Charlie Brown?

Give Linus and Snoopy a trusty
blanket to snuggle with.

Time to beat the heat!
Draw a place where everyone can go swimming.

Charlie Brown is unwrapping a present!
What's inside?

What is Franklin catching?

Fore! Put some clubs in Charlie Brown's golf bag.

Linus has found the Great Pumpkin!
What does it look like?

Marcie and Peppermint Patty are looking at a cool poster. What is on it?

Charlie Brown missed the ball again.
Maybe a hat will help him block out the sun.

Ring, ring! Who is Lucy talking to?

What does the pot at the end of the rainbow hold?

Decorate Snoopy's doghouse for the holidays.

Why is everyone waiting in line?
And what are they traveling with?

What is Lucy giving Linus?

Lucy and Linus are off to school!
Give them backpacks, lunches,
and anything else they need.

Marcie and Peppermint Patty look chilly! Give them a fire to warm their hands over.

Go fish! Draw Snoopy and Rerun
some cards so they can play.

Peppermint Patty doesn't look too happy!
What's in the water?

Linus's snowman needs some accessories! Doodle him some gloves, a hat, buttons, and a face.

Peppermint Patty is in the mood for a snack.
What is she eating?

Finders keepers! What did Sally find underneath the bed?

What are Charlie Brown and his friends selling at their stand?

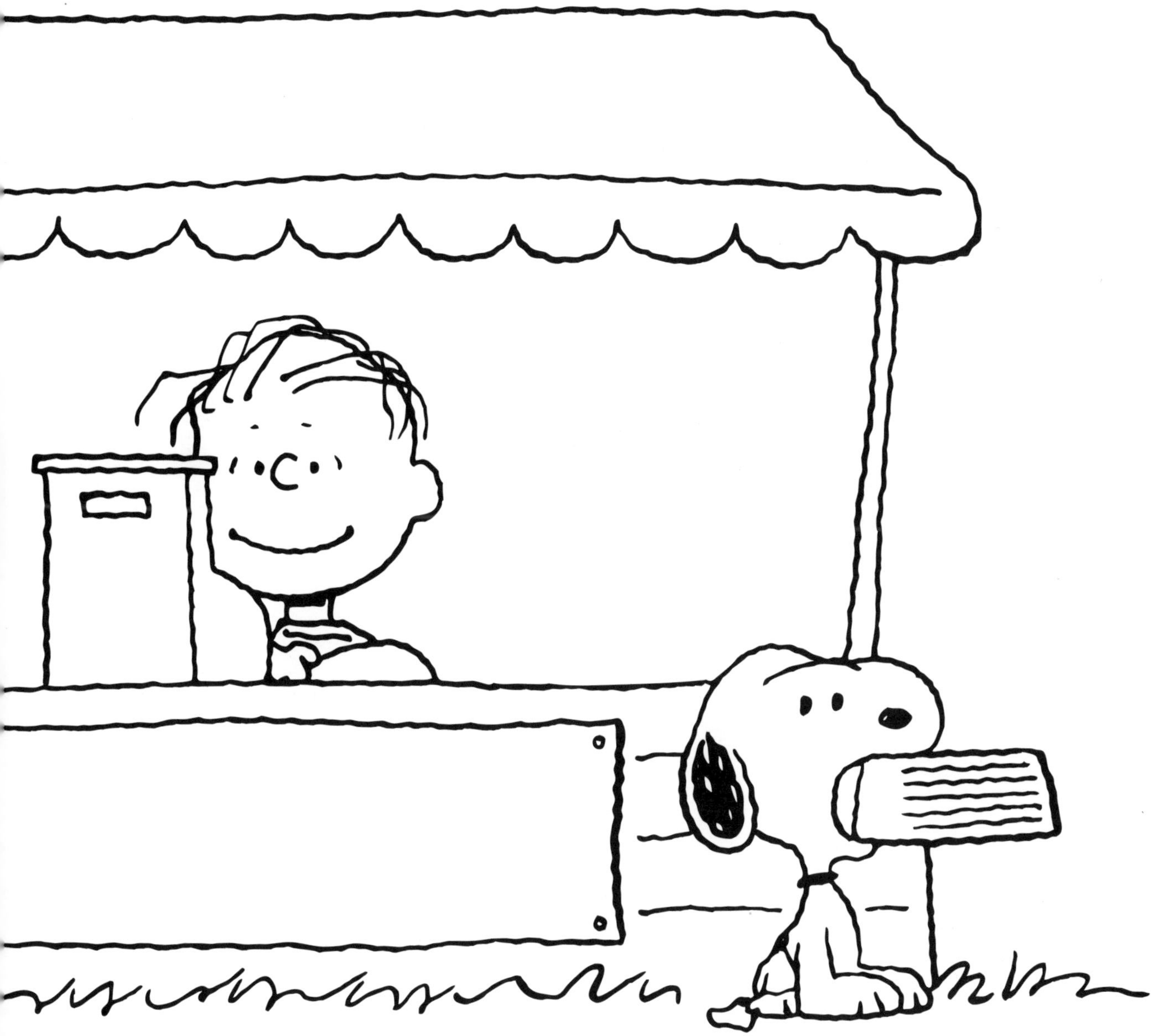

Who is Charlie Brown sitting with on the couch?

Charlie Brown and Linus are on their way to school.
How will they get there?

Rerun wants to play! Give him a ball and a basket.

The Flying Ace and Peppermint Patty are out for a quick flight! What do they see up in the air?

Lucy is being nice and giving Rerun a toy. What is it?

Voilà! Complete Peppermint Patty's work of art.

Woodstock is taking in the sun!
What does he need to stay cool?

How is Charlie Brown's scarf decorated?